Mig the Pig

Colin and Jacqui Hawkins

PUFFIN BOOKS

Do you know Mig the pig?

Mig the pig is very big.

She likes to wear a bright red wig.

W

Mig often goes riding in her gig.

One day while out in her gig,
Mig stopped for a dig.

d

But the wind blew her red wig onto a twig.

Mig shook the twig and down came her wig along with a fig.

Now she has a wig

...and a fig.

So happy was Mig to get back
her red wig, along with a fig
that she danced a wild jig.

What will Mig ...do with
her fig?

Then home in the gig to bake the fig went the pig called Mig.

Some Other Picture Puffins